W9-AQM-939

0 1021 0183333 7

ON LINE

The Life and Work of...

Jackson Pollock

Leonie Bennett

Heinemann Library
Chicago, Illinois

© 2005 Heinemann Library
Published by Heinemann Library, a division of Reed Elsevier, Inc.
Chicago, Illinois
Customer Service 888-363-4266
Visit our website at www.heinemannlibrary.com

Library of Congress Cataloging-in-Publication Data:
Bennett, Leonie.
    Jackson Pollock / Leonie Bennett.
       p. cm. -- (Life and work of--)
    Includes bibliographical references and index.
    ISBN 1-4034-5073-0 (library binding) -- ISBN 1-4034-5562-7 (pbk.)
    1. Pollock, Jackson, 1912-1956--Juvenile literature. 2.
    Painters--United States--Biography--Juvenile literature. I. Title.
    II. Series.

ND237.P73B46 2004
759.13--dc22

                                        2004014058

Printed and bound by South China Printing Company, China

08 07 06 05
10 9 8 7 6 5 4 3 2 1

Acknowledgments
The author and publishers are grateful to the following for permission to reproduce copyright material:
Corbis/Burckhardt Rudolph/Corbis Sygma/ARS, NY and DACS, London 2004 p. 4, 16, 22; Art Institute of Chicago/ARS, NY and DACS, London 2004 p. 17; Bridgeman Art Library/Peggy Guggenheim Collection, Venice/ARS, NY and DACS, London 2004 p. 19; Bridgeman Art Library/Private Collection/ARS, NY and DACS, London 2004 pp. 7, 13; Bridgeman Art Library/ National Gallery of Art, Washington DC/ARS, NY and DACS, London 2004 p. 5; Corbis/Burckhardt Rudolph/Corbis Sygma/ARS, NY and DACS, London 2004 p. 24; Guggenheim Museum / ARS,NY and DACS, London 2004 p. 27; Hulton pp. 14; 24; Joslyn Art Museum/ARS, NY and DACS, London 2004 p. 21; Martha Holmes/Time Life Pictures/Getty Images p. 18; Museum of Modern Art, New York © 2003, Digital Image, The Museum of Modern Art, New York/Scala, Firenze/ARS, NY and DACS, London 2004 pp. 11, 15, 25; Pollock-Krasner House and Study Center, East Hampton, NY pp. 6, 9, 26; The Metropolitan Museum of Art, George A.Hearn Fund, 1957, (57.92)/ ARS, NY and DACS, London 2004 p. 23.

Cover painting (*White Light*, 1954) reproduced with permission of Corbis/Francis G. Mayer/ARS, NY and DACS, London 2004.

Contents

Any words appearing in the text in bold, **like this**, are explained in the Glossary.

Who was Jackson Pollock?

Jackson Pollock was one of the best-known American artists of the 20th century. He lived and worked in New York in the 1940s and 1950s.

Jackson is famous for his "drip" paintings. They are full of wild movement and crazy patterns. He made them by dripping paint on a **canvas**.

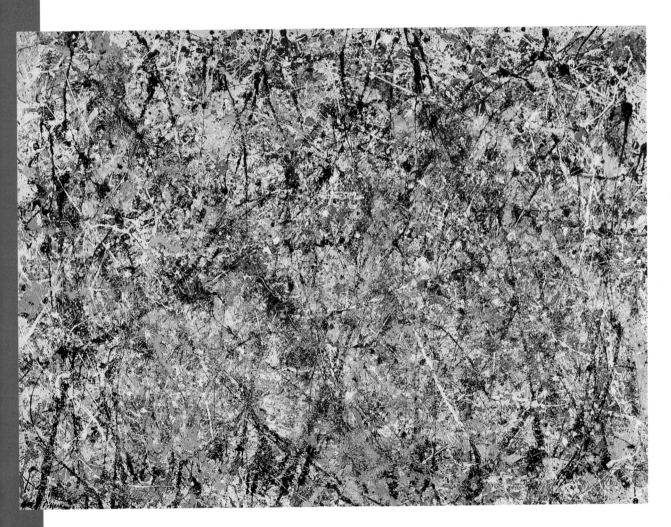

Lavender Mist: Number 1, 1950

Early Years

Jackson was born on January 28, 1912, in the state of Wyoming. His family moved around the country looking for work. By the time he was ten he had lived in six homes.

When Jackson was nine his father left home to work. Jackson lived with his mother and four brothers. When Jackson was sad he drew and painted to make himself feel better.

Self portrait,
1931

School and College

Sometimes Jackson's sadness made him angry. He got into trouble at school. When he went to college to study art he was **expelled** for bad behavior.

As a young man, Jackson **sketched** objects and people. He also copied great works of art from the past. His mother **encouraged** him. She wanted him to become an artist.

New York

When he was eighteen, Jackson went to New York. He worked as a cleaner and a **lumberjack** to make money, but he wanted to be a painter.

Jackson joined a group of other artists, painting **murals**. He also did his own **abstract** paintings. It was hard to recognize objects or people in them.

The Flame, 1934–38

A Turning Point

Jackson was very unhappy. In 1938 he was fired from his job. At last he began to work harder on his own paintings.

In 1941, Jackson saw an **exhibition** of **Native American** art. He became interested in their stories and artwork. This painting shows the "Moon-Woman" from a Native American story.

The Moon-Woman, 1942

Selling His Work

In 1942, Jackson met Peggy Guggenheim. Peggy had a **gallery** called The Art of this Century. She showed only **modern** paintings and **sculptures**.

Peggy sold Jackson's work in her gallery. He had his first **solo exhibition** there in 1943. Some people thought this picture was the best in the show.

Stenographic Figure, 1942

Marriage

Jackson had met an artist called Lee Krasner. They got married in 1945 and went to live on a farm outside New York city.

Jackson was much happier living with Lee. She helped him to work better. Jackson did this painting in one of the upstairs bedrooms of the farmhouse.

The Key, 1946

Action Painting

Jackson didn't plan his paintings or **sketch** out his ideas first. He covered the **canvas** with marks and colors without thinking.

Jackson kept moving the whole time he worked. This is called action painting. The paintings often give us a feeling of movement.

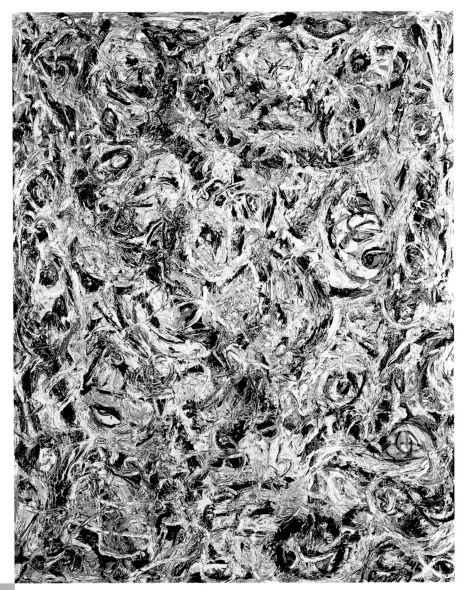

Eyes in the Heat, 1946

19

Painting on the Floor

Jackson liked the way **Native American** artists poured sand on the ground to make patterns. Jackson put his **canvas** on the floor. Then he poured paint onto the canvas.

Jackson stopped using paintbrushes. He moved the paint around with sticks or knives. Sometimes he added sand or broken glass. This gave the paintings more **texture**.

Galaxy, 1947

Drip Paintings

Around 1947, Jackson started making "drip" paintings. He worked very fast, dripping paint from a stick or brush. He walked all around the **canvas** while he worked.

The painting is a **record** of all of his movements. It is also a record of his feelings. Jackson said that **modern** artists painted their feelings instead of the world outside.

Autumn Rhythm (Number 30), 1950

Famous

By 1949 Jackson was famous. Some people said that he was the greatest living painter in the United States. Others hated his paintings. They thought they were just a mess.

But Jackson was still not happy. He stopped giving his paintings **titles** because they were not pictures of anything. Sometimes he just gave them numbers.

One (Number 31, 1950)

A Sad End

Jackson died in a car crash on August 11, 1956. He was only 44. Later that year, there was a big **exhibition** of his work in New York.

Some of Jackson's last paintings show faces and **figures**. But had been too unhappy to paint many pictures in the last few years of his life.

Ocean Greyness, 1953

Timeline

1912	Paul Jackson Pollock is born in Wyoming on January 28.
1913–24	The Pollocks move back and forth between Arizona and California.
1921	Jackson's father, LeRoy Pollock, gets a job away from home.
1926	Jackson enrolls in Manual Arts training school.
1929	Jackson is **expelled** from Manual Arts for bad behavior.
1930	Jackson moves to New York where he lives with his brother, Charles.
1930-35	Jackson works as a cleaner and a **lumberjack**. He is very poor. He paints *Self portrait*.
1934–38	Jackson paints *The Flame*.
1935	Jackson joins the Federal Arts Project—mural division.
1938	Jackson loses his job with the Federal Arts Project because he is often misses work.
1939	Jackson sees an **exhibition** of Picasso's work.
1941	Jackson meets Lee Krasner. Jackson sees an exhibition of Native American art.
1942	Jackson paints *The Moon-Woman* and *Stenographic Figure*. Jackson meets Peggy Guggenheim.
1943	Jackson has his first **solo exhibition**. Peggy agrees to pay him $150 per month so that he can paint full time.

1944	Jackson sells a painting to a museum for the first time. The Museum of **Modern** Art in New York buys *The She-Wolf*.
1945	Jackson and Lee marry and move to the country.
1946	Jackson paints *Eyes in the Heat* and *The Key*.
1947	Jackson begins making "drip" paintings. He paints *Galaxy*.
1950	Hans Namuth photographs and films Jackson as he works. Jackson paints *Lavender Mist: Number 1, Autumn Rhythm* and *One (Number 31)*.
1953	Jackson paints *Ocean Greyness*.
1954	Jackson paints very little.
1956	Jackson has not painted in almost 18 months. He dies in a car accident on August 11.

Glossary

abstract art that deals with ideas rather than the way things look

Native American people who lived in North America before the Europeans arrived

canvas material on which pictures are often painted

encourage give hope and confidence to somebody

exhibition show of art for the public

expelled forced to leave a school or college

figure the shape of a person

gallery room or building where art is shown

lumberjack person who chops down trees

modern recent

mural picture painted on to a wall

record pattern that shows evidence

sculpture art that is not flat—often made of wood, stone, or metal

sketch rough drawing

solo one person only

texture the way something feels if you touch it—such as smooth, rough, or lumpy

title the name given to something

Find Out More

Paintings to see

The Moon-Woman. 1942. Guggenheim Museum, New York.

Cathedral. 1947. Dallas Museum of Art.

Number 10, 1949. 1949. Museum of Fine Arts, Boston.

Number 1, 1950 (Lavender Mist). 1950. National Gallery of Art, Washington, D.C.

One (Number 31, 1950). 1950. The Museum of Modern Art, New York.

Books to read

Clare Oliver. *Artists in Their Time: Jackson Pollock*. New York: Scholastic, Franklin Watts, 2003.

Jan Greenberg and Sandra Jordon. *Action Jackson*. Brookfield, Conneticut: Millbrook Press, Roaring Book, 2002.

Mike Venezia. *Getting to Know the World's Greatest Artists: Jackson Pollock*. New York: Franklin Watts, 1999.

Index